a commoner's prayer

poems

by
Joan M. White

Montpelier, VT

a commoner's prayer: poems
©2025 by Joan M. White

Release Date: April 1, 2026

All Rights Reserved. Printed in the USA.

Paperback ISBN: 978-1-57869-220-0

Library of Congress Control Number: 2026901375

Published by Rootstock Publishing
an imprint of Ziggy Media, LLC
Montpelier, VT 05602

info@rootstockpublishing.com
www.rootstockpublishing.com

Book design by Eddie Vincent, ENC Graphic Services.

Cover photo (rhododendron in winter) and author photo by Emily Cross, www.ecrossphoto.com.

No AI training. No part of this book may be reproduced or transmitted in any form or by any means, electronic or mechanical, including photocopying, recording, or by an information storage and retrieval system (except by a journalist or reviewer who may quote brief passages in an academic or editorial review) without permission in writing.

For reprint permissions, or to schedule a book club visit or author reading, contact Joan at Agapitajwhite@gmail.com.

"This luminous collection offers poems of immediacy and depth. With a disarming naturalness that belies the depth of knowledge of poetic tradition, of the world, and of Zen that this poet clearly possesses—(R.H. Blyth wrote, "Without Zen there is no poetry and without poetry there is no Zen.")—each of these brief poems has the power to return us to a richer vision of this very life, just as it is. Reading them I found myself surprised, delighted, and grateful."

—Rafe Martin, author of *Rough-Faced Girl*

"Joan White's common/uncommon poems exist in 'the little hour/crossing the border from life to story/and back again.' It's that *little* hour that makes her journey so remarkable, so alive. She is kin to the 17th century Japanese poet Bashō, who in his masterful haibun *The Narrow Road to the Interior*, blurs traditional distinctions of poetry and prose, of external and internal worlds. In her own stunning haibun, White moves between ways of looking at the world, between everyday speech and elegance. She infuses scientific factoids with the mystery of a Zen koan. This collection is rich, full of journeys ranging from meditations on global migration to tender family memories to wildfires and floods and the fall of democracy—but White reminds us that flowers changed the world. *a commoner's prayer* is a gem, full of spirit and love, of celebration, of yearning, of common sense."

—Sue D. Burton, author of *BOX*

"Buddha said, 'If we could see the miracle of a single flower clearly our whole lives would change.' In *a commoner's prayer* Joan White leads us toward this kind of revelation. Through her patient, contemplative inquiry we are taken from the whorl of a 6,000-year-old shell to the physical pain of the global pandemic—from the bud of a rhododendron to the origin of human kind—from a button on a tattered coat to the heart of a family. With tender observations and diligent curiosity, White's poems speak to the balance between patience and urgency so critical to our times. These poems of desire and awe guide us to the miracle of deep connection in the vast universe of everyday life."

—Alison Prine, author of *Loss and Its Antonym*

for Jonan and Ian

Contents

common prayer 1

MIGRATION 5
UNDERTAKING 6
A TREE TREEING 7
MONUMENT 8
SUCH STUFF AS DREAMS 10
NATURAL HISTORY 11
SPORES WREAK HAVOC IN THE NEIGHBORHOOD 12
THE EPIPHYTIC CACTUS TRAPPED IN A CLAY POT FOR A DECADE BLOOMS 13
BELONGING 14
NIGHT MUSIC 15

common prayer 19

LETTER TO BASHO 23
HOMO SAPIEN INUNDATUS 24
ENCOUNTERING THE MAIDEN NEVER SAD AT TRADER JOE'S ... 25
WHY THE WORLD IS SO BLUE 26
COLCHESTER BOG 27
MAKE A WISH 28
FIREFLIES 29
FLOAT 30
TRANSLATION 31
DANDELION 32
THE FLOWER CARRIER 33
CLOUD BANK 34
JULY 35

common prayer 39

LETTER TO COLD MOUNTAIN 43
TROWEL 44
SMALL HISTORIES *for Ellie* 45
WRECKAGE 46
DAY OF THE DEAD for Shawn 47
FOR DARK TIMES 48
RED MAPLES 49
HOW TO HYPNOTIZE A CHICKEN 50
OCTOBER TOMATO 51
LABOR DAY (with a line from Su Tung-P'o) 52
ECLIPSE 53

common prayer 57

NORTHERN LIGHTS 61
RHODODENDRON, WINTER 62
DAILY BREAD 63
LAID LOW WITH COVID, I PONDER THE LIGHTNING WHELK
    SHELL ON THE BOOKCASE 64
MY MOTHER'S COAT 65
RUE THIS DAY 66
AT THE APPROACH OF THE WINTER SOLSTICE 67
MOURNING 68
GOOD JOURNALISM TELLS US WHO, WHAT,
    WHEN, WHERE, AND WHY 69
A PLEA 70

common prayer 73

IN THE BEGINNING 77
WE'VE LOST TRACK OF OUR MOTHER 78
DIRGE 79
OUT OF SIGHT, OUT OF MIND 80
BOOKMARK 81
TINY APOCALYPSE 82
MEMORY'S MUSCLE 83
PLOUGHSHARE TORTOISE 84
ADVOCATING FOR THE INCONCEIVEABLE 85
a commoner's prayer 86
GONE 87

NOTES 91
ACKNOWLEDGMENTS 92
ABOUT THE AUTHOR 93

common prayer

Between cloud and rain there's a burden.
Between seed and sprout there's a breach.
The field of dirt greens and greens.

It's the little hour,
crossing the border from life to story
and back again.

MIGRATION

Leaving the Great Rift Valley
where were you going

no shoes, no map, no road
not even a country to call home

and what did you carry
other than a few words, some tools

migrating through the years
all the way to Tierra del Fuego

passing down your dreams
from two hundred to billions

your penchant for art
iron oxide on cave walls

where you'd rest your head at night
worrying a stone in your hand

not tomorrow
as you drifted off to sleep

UNDERTAKING

A break in the bark and the scent is unleashed,
alerting the beetles to fresh flesh.

They arrive in their camouflage suits: one or two, soon hundreds.
Jewel and bark beetles, longhorns, pine borers.

Listen for them chewing as you make your way along the trail.
A higher pitch on warm days. White noise.

Tiny tombs of sawdust rise from the forest floor
below their drilled doorways—entrances to the inner cambium.

Each hole leads to a nuptial chamber.
Drilling another gallery, she lays her eggs,

and the feeding frenzy begins—
the larvae's scribbled epitaphs like brittle snowflakes.

Fungus and bacteria speed the undertaking.
Buds bursting, leaves unfurling,

this is what it's like to be eaten alive.

A TREE TREEING

Choosing one, it would have to be the beech tree at my elementary school. Humongous limbs branching out low enough for a first grader to make a start. Branches wide enough to lie down on and take a nap. At 200 years old, an ancient beast in our linear time scheme, but a mere adolescent next to the Bristle Cones or Redwoods that understand the world after thousands of years. That's what I want—the kind of knowledge that makes you fearless. A kind of fearlessness that manifests as acceptance as the tiniest creatures overcome you. And to welcome them— the woodpecker's knock, carpenter ants, the larvae's lunch. Aphids amassing by the thousands. And the final fall—trunk and branches cracking, plummeting through yet other trunks, branches, twigs, and coming to rest among the leaves and litter of the forest. Come spring, new life sprouts along the tree's body in the kind-of straight line we'd try to make in elementary school.

wood a very rare/substance in the universe/requires life to exist

MONUMENT

Each day after the builders went home
she drew out her black marker
and covered the struts and beams of
her unfinished home with words:
The world is a flower. Gods are flowers.
All phenomena are flowers.

And when they put up the dry wall, painted
and finished the job, you couldn't see
red flowers, white flowers, green flowers, black flowers.

She never spoke of them
just as she never did of him
and his short life.

Family and friends who came to visit spoke
of children and work and politics.
They ate and drank and laughed
while kids screamed down the hallways
unaware of flowers within the walls.

Sometimes one would run a finger
along the wood trim,
or lean against a wall tying their shoe.
You were born out of these flowers,
you gave birth to these flowers.

And in summer, beyond the house
a field filled with white marguerites and pink phlox,

and drifts of dewy milkweed in the fall.

These she spoke of
though they were laced with spider webs,
lifting in the breeze and falling
where they were attached.

And when the snow came to steal the field
she built a bonfire of oak logs in the center,
asking the sun to return.

She bought a bouquet of lilies,
and arranged them in a vase on the table—
their trumpets trumpeting his presence everywhere.

SUCH STUFF AS DREAMS

It's the worldliness of the world
that troubles me.
How the leaves cling to the tree even as they fall.
The way the monarch caterpillar
holds onto the milkweed,
struggling to shed its skin.
Fog grips the mountains and hills as it lifts.
I found a small red rock in the La Platte River
and crushed it using another—
stone upon stone—
until it was a tiny pile of red clay.
Mixed it with some river water
palmed it into a ball and tossed it back.
This morning, I collected
the tiger lilies' black seeds,
put them in a plastic sandwich bag
in the fridge.
They need the cold and dark
to germinate in the spring.
We dream this world into being
with our words.
Rain strikes the apple blossoms
and butterflies take flight.

NATURAL HISTORY

I want to sit for a while and remember the whole wide world—
how flowers changed it, the firefly's burden.

When I set out, I had no idea how thin the air
would be under my feet. Like trying to hold onto

the piece of amethyst I found at Blomidon Point.
Put it in my pocket, then gave it a place

in my natural history collection. Shuffled it into a drawer.
Now I'm almost somewhere

and I turn it over and over in my hand—
this emptiness that won't let go.

My sister says rocks grow. But I'm wondering about
evolution—the one no one sees

until everything is different. Like the flowering plants,
their appearance in the world still a mystery.

Suddenly everywhere—
their seeds winged yet grasping.

SPORES WREAK HAVOC IN THE NEIGHBORHOOD

Spores of apple-cedar rust
lurk in the debris under the juniper,
waiting for an animal's scratch and claw,
the wind's breath and lift.
I know this having seen orange goo
clinging to the tree's limbs last summer.
A host?
Half an hour at the garden center
inquiring about the tree's downfall,
I returned to twisted black galls.

Instructed to wait until spring,
now I'm in the shed hunting down fungicide,
else the neighbor's apple tree bears the news
as blotched yellow leaves,
apples dimpled and scabbed and mutated.

Dreams of jam and pie blindsided,
the owners scout the neighborhood
for the perpetrator.

The garden and its ruse.
My curtains drawn, no one sees me
sitting at the kitchen table, slicing an apple,
chomping it down.

THE EPIPHYTIC CACTUS TRAPPED IN A CLAY POT FOR A DECADE BLOOMS

On again—the great game of seeking the secret of the universe as the Large Hadron Collider fires up and resumes shooting protons around a 17-mile electromagnetic underground racetrack. Scientists seeking answers to questions a set of equations can't quite grasp: *Where did the universe come from? Why is it matter, not anti-matter? What is dark matter?* Protons crashing, sparks of primordial energy flying, fizzing electrons. What about the sound? Ghostly neurons, wobbling muons. B quarks. B for bottom, or perhaps beauty. The beauty in my living room an epiphytic cactus, blooming. Epi for "upon," as in cliff, or tree branch, or where you planted your wishes as a child. I took three cuttings from a friend's plant, dipped them in rooting hormone, planted the trio in soil. Waited. Ten Years. As slow as a star rebounding from a black hole a pink phallic-like bud births a fuchsia flower large enough to fill my hand. A galaxy of stamens orbits the pistil crowned with a miniscule white star. Come closer. Lend it your ear.

BELONGING

Dusk belongs to the woodcock—
peent, peent, a nasally bugle call
beyond the stand of rogue box elders.
The bird flutters skyward in
wide spirals—up and up and up
toward Venus, cavorting
with the crescent moon.
The spirals steeper and tighter
until a speck in the night sky
tumbles like a crippled plane,
comes in for a soft landing where it began.
Twilight's brief secrets.
The sound of heavy breathing.
Curious, I open the door,
put the light on
to find a black bear
taking down the bird feeder.
I clap my hands, tell it to go home
as if this world belongs to me.
It's a standoff—the beast backs off a few feet,
light glinting off its eyes,
as it glares at the feeder.
I do what one does in the grip of darkness—
close the door.

NIGHT MUSIC

We cannot kill the night with our sleep—
white astilbes light the path
down to the lake where the fireflies'
questions reflect too softly on the water for
bats to answer.

What is the hurry toward daylight?
Let night be what it is.

Let bull frogs tune up their bass strings
to the plucking of green ones
as the knot of tree toads unravels its trill.

Let's sit on the wet grass where night has
needled its way between each blade and
invite the dark to slip between our toes and fingers,
rest under our elbows and knees.

Why close the door, turn on the lights?
This is our music too.

common prayer

Sleep turns to torpor turns to waking.
It's the first hour.

Paws at my face.
Nibbles at my mind.

Converses with ghosts.
Scribbles a litany of tasks.

I throw them off with the covers.

LETTER TO BASHO

startled by the crow's
winged shadow at my two feet
reverie arrives

and I wonder
did you track the seasons
by the lengthening of your shadow

as you made your way
on the long journey to the interior

the two of you resting on a stone wall
sucking on a plum pit
before entering the poetry
of a village

and did your illness tighten its grip
during the hours of words

until all that was left of your syllables
was their specter
drifting through the valley

caw! caw! caw! caw! caw!
the crow perching above me
cocks its head to hear

HOMO SAPIEN INUNDATUS

July in Vermont
10 inches of rain
11 inches of rain
12 inches of rain
we are inundatus
of places that flood
says the botanical
rivers devour banks
small towns, islands
books and boughs
float down main street
cornfields—swampland
hayfields—black mold
green moss abounds
tulip tree blooms
out of season
globe flower too
slugs feast on dahlias
oyster mushrooms
on iris tubers
a tiny orchid
rises above debris
symbiotic
with fungus
Epipactis helleborine
epipactis
for curdled milk
hellebore
from the Greek
'helein,' *to injure*
noxious
are we?

ENCOUNTERING THE MAIDEN NEVER SAD AT TRADER JOE'S

> *The beautiful Lady Lu*
> *long ago was called Never Sad...*
> *she knelt on a green bear rug*
> *and wore a blue phoenix robe...*
>
> —The Collected Songs of Cold Mountain, 46
> Translated by Red Pine

She bursts through the doors
at Trader Joe's, her wild gestures
boiling over her entourage,
her laughter drowning the silent
business of everyday shoppers.
Hair tucked into a beanie,
shimmering with rhinestones
and made in China, torn blue jeans
in Vietnam, running shoes too,
blue t-shirt with a black crow
rising between her breasts,
rising again with her gesticulating arms
to expose a bare belly. She kneels
to smell the roses jetted all the way
from Panama, tosses a dozen purple
into her shopping cart,
then fruit and cheese and nuts,
a bottle of Merlot,
some bread to break with friends.
Rides the wave of her joy through the aisles,
stopping her carriage short at the chocolate bars.
Some 60%, some 75%
cocoa from Cote D'Ivoire.
Her laughter floats down the aisles
and landing on my shoulders,
my knees buckle
under the weight of desire.

WHY THE WORLD IS SO BLUE

There is no blue sky or ocean.
No blue morpho butterfly—
a creature colluding with light.
Not even bluejays.
Hold a feather up to the sun—
the blue disappears.

In this world there are no perfect circles.
At their circumference lies impermanence—
particles, cells, atoms in constant motion.

Centrifugal force causes a bulge
at the Earth's equator.
The orb drawn on a blackboard falls short.
NASA's quartz gyroscopic rotors,
the most precise man-made spheres ever,
less than three ten-millionths of an inch from ideal.

In this world we seek permanence.
Our disappointment like the blue water
rippling outward from a pebble tossed in a lake—
almost perfect.

COLCHESTER BOG

Somewhat lost, I ended up in a suburban neighborhood where a neighborly woman gave me what she thought to be poor directions that took me to a boardwalk and the beauty of a ruined world—small boggy islands wreathed in a tangle of tamarack, swamp azalea, bog rosemary. Gazing skyward at a young larch, I almost missed it among the roots and muck and moss and water that spring had rained upon us—a nest of pitcher plants. Mouths wide open, hungering for more.

A nest of babies/stir at the slightest movement/of their mother's wings

MAKE A WISH

After supper,
we covered ourselves with a blanket
to keep mosquitos at bay,
and laid on our backs in the field
below the cemetery,

our gaze following the arc to Arcturus,
speeding on to Spica—
asterisks in the night sky,
standing in for omitted matter.

An annotation speaking to us
in the ASKII language:
42=asterisk=anything you want it to be.

FIREFLIES

It was a longing for the stars'
Perfect alignment
Brought me to
This field
This night
Seeking the fallen
As they cascaded one after another
Onto the somber soil
And I cupped them between my palms.

FLOAT

First in the amniotic fluid—
cacophony of existence muffled
by skin and sac.

Then on Pimlico Pond
her hand at my five-year-old back.
A rare moment with a mother of eight.

But that day at the town pool:
six-year-old me in the deepest water,
I slipped under.
Rose and gasped and thrashed
my way to a swim instructor's hand.

Having failed the swimming test,
furious, I ran home to tell her,
for her to hold me,
bathe me in her sympathy.
And her question:
Why didn't you float?

This summer day on Lake Champlain
floating in the fractured light,
empty blue sky before me,
Andromeda Galaxy moving
toward us,
I say, *hold me.*

TRANSLATION

after Cheryl Betz's "Echinoides II (Isle Au Haut)"

I was trying to understand the Latin
when the sea urchin's spiky crown
emerged in the sky,
circling its way around and through
the pine's dark branches and needles.
Two creatures, two worlds
remembering each other—
an ecstatic dance.
In memory's distance, a barefoot girl arose,
sea urchin in hand.
& another, climbing,
grasping the bark and branches—
bare foot following bare foot.
& I understood
the tongue of earth and salt.

DANDELION

A glistening of goldfinch
on the lawn
feasting on dandelion seeds
know something about goodness
we do not.

THE FLOWER CARRIER

after Diego Rivera's "The Flower Carrier, 1935"

Serious business, these flowers.
Each one filled with the toil of Earth
Sun and Water. The flower carrier is kneeling

his dark hands splayed against the ground
the earth's musk before him.
Petals caress his hat

as the woman ties the basket
of pink, red, purple and orange flowers
on his back.

He can't see his burden, only feels
its weight shift. Their mass of yellow centers
crest the basket's horizon.

They rise and fall in a soft hush
with each step the flower carrier takes
to the market, where their perfume rises

above fish, swine and fowl
the vendors' cacophony.
Women in long skirts and shawls

of pink, red, purple and orange
gather around the basket's crown of jewels
picking out small bunches

they carry swiftly home
to altars laden with memories—
the burden of flowers.

CLOUD BANK

in memory of Marylen

This greenhouse world cups the cheek
of blue sky in its sweaty palm

and cumulus clouds blossom into fat old men
sitting in straight-backed chairs,

smoking exotic blends of pipe tobacco,
curlicues rising and erasing themselves.

Their stubby fingers lift steaming cups of coffee,
and who knows what is smoke or steam or man,

hanging over the lake,
where a child stands on the shore

pointing at the clouds' story—
the one nobody wants to hear.

JULY

arrives a little later
each morning, same *O-Ka-Lee* of redwings
same azure sky, a few veteran clouds
from last night's storm.
I share some cream with the cat
pouring mine over raspberries
and we eat breakfast at the picnic table.
European honeybees caress the clover,
yellow jackets and deer flies fight
over fruit and blood.
The neighbor's lawn mower gasps and hums.
Across the road, the community of
Queen Anne's lace and blue asters gather
along the shoulder waving their heads
like children with flags at the parade.
A celebration of the courage
to sustain the dialectic
between the government & the governed.
They are not concerned with red & blue,
left & right.
Just the urgency of the season
and the wind's collusion.

common prayer

In the midst of the day, a repast.
Rising from the table,
thoughts flood in
while crumbs linger on the plate.

I wet my forefinger
& relish in their capture.

LETTER TO COLD MOUNTAIN

Let us meet at Tientai
where the herb gatherers
entered the forest,
returning 200 years later.
Let us both come as we are,
two brushes and a big pot of ink.
Let us duel, slopping our black diction
on the face of a sheer rock wall
until we run dry. Having said it all.
Having said nothing.
Let the rains come,
and our words fall
through the cataract,
slowing at the crevasse
where you once disappeared,
and landing in a ravine,
flow into stream after stream.
Along the way,
gathering all the chatter
from this world of dust
and with it enter the Yangtze,
that empties into the China Sea at Huangchou,
where the two of us float belly up
and wash our ears out.

TROWEL

I keep a red-handled one close.
Its round tip chipped on one side
and worn smooth.
Bodhidharma had a broken tooth.
In October, his red and gold robes
drift down the mountains
into the valleys.
Maple, oak, and birch
giving way to the cold nights.
It's said that he tore his eyelids off,
not wanting to sleep, but to wake.
His eyes like full moons,
flecked with the detritus of human suffering.
I want to call October's the Trowel Moon.
I want to translate the cricket's song.
I want to dig a good hole.

SMALL HISTORIES

for Ellie

You say you caught yourself wondering if
the world would be
when you were gone.

Rumpled bed sheets rumpled bed sheets.
The sound of a small brass bell to ring for help
the sound of a small brass bell.

Hair comb in hand at the ready
to fix the damage from hands patting your head.

I wonder why
the vase of ranunculus and baby's breath
sits on the kitchen counter.
You ask about images
of a woman floating behind me.

We spend the hour reciting small histories.

I ask about the light. What color.
Gold, you say,
pointing at the carpet of gingko leaves,
falling throughout the day.
Grateful we don't rake them up.

WRECKAGE

After the storm I walk,
listening to the leaves' muted voices.

Descend the broken paths
clambering over fallen trees.

Peer inside the windthrown—cool & dark,
the rabbit's eyes flashing.

Storm raging outside,
my childhood-self feasted on that fright—

glued to the window,
black pupils spilling across my eyes,

nausea rising from my belly.
Wishing for felled trees

in the woods behind the house,
I sought out the wounded,

escaped my howling clan
& rested in the womb of damp soil.

Wreckage all around me—
green and trembling.

DAY OF THE DEAD

for Shawn

Time falls backward one hour
and the dark closes in early,
slinking between every branch and twig,
every blade of grass.
Frost prowls right up to daybreak.

Mornings,
I find the headless bodies of mice
left on the bed by the cat.

Boxelder and ambush beetles
slip into the living room through cracks
I cannot see.

Given the chance, wolf spiders lurking
by the back door scurry into the mudroom.

But it's the witch hazel's shock
of gold tentacle-like blossoms
takes my breath away.

Wych from the old English—*to bend*.
Water that once pulsed from root to crown
tugs the cut branches in the dowser's hands
earthward.

It's the Day of the Dead—
the veil between your world and mine,
thin.

Closing my eyes,
I take your hands in mine.
Pull you toward me.

FOR DARK TIMES

I'm on my knees
foraging for cones under the scotch pine
behind Jimmo's Motel.
Comb the shore of Lake Champlain for still more.
At Red Rocks, hundreds of acorns
crunch under my feet.
At an abandoned house on Shelburne Road,
Douglas fir.
My neighbors don't mind my hunger
for their blue spruce and balsam,
white and Mugo pine.
For dark times,
I make a wreath. A crown.
Not all come down to jewels or thorns.
Nor Apollo's glossy laurel.
To melt the pitch, to make them shine,
I put them in the oven.
Wiring the cones bloodies the hands,
so I pull on a pair of gloves.
Divide the circle in thirds
with pinion pine turned on their backs
showing off their Fibonacci spirals.
Distribute the cones
equally among the three. Finished,
I bring it outdoors. Hang it
from a tree branch.
Let the squirrels and chipmunks and finches
feast upon it.

RED MAPLES

That's me, the skinny girl
standing at the top of a bare tree
in the Edward Gorey print.
The tree not much more than a stick.

From here I can see the curvature of the earth.
And the air, lifting my stringy hair,
carries the steely scent of snow.
Sticking out my tongue to catch the flavor,
it vanishes.

When I put my ear to the sky
the ringing of a school bell
collides with the strident cry of a crow.

From here, the world is vast and empty,
broken by a stand of red maples—
Red buds in spring followed by red flowers.
Red leaves in fall.
Red branches in winter.
More a heart than a tree.

It's dark now and I'm keeping watch
to see if the world dismantles itself while we sleep.
But there's always someone, somewhere
conjuring the other.

HOW TO HYPNOTIZE A CHICKEN

In the reception line, meeting my sister's eyes,
I see that she has shrunk. She says *it should be me
in that box.* I think to myself *the corpse should never be
your daughter.* Music from her wedding day makes us cry,
the chaplain is a stranger, and 100 white roses standing upright
in a square, sent by her husband's colleagues, resemble a grave.
My sister says *Wasn't it beautiful?* Nodding, we
all agree. And at the reception at Moose Lodge why
does our cousin Tommy feel the need to share how he
learned from his dad who learned from our grandfather how to
hypnotize a chicken? Then his charade of drawing a straight line
in the dirt and setting the bird down in front of it to see.
The bird struck dumb and falling into a trance.
All of us laughing so hard it hurt.

OCTOBER TOMATO

I wanted the last one before frost took it. Not red enough. I wanted it simple—sliced and salted. So I risked it. Mexican by origin. Botanically a fruit. Culinarily a vegetable. Spanish colonists introduced them to North America in the 17th century. Early Americans had very strong opinions about the correct color of food. Red was not one of them. No one thought about eating tomatoes. 1838—the Tomato Pill War ensued—*Dr. Miles Compound Extract of Tomato* claiming to cure everything from indigestion to syphilis challenged by Dr. Guy Phelps' *Compound Tomato Pills*. Both men claiming theirs the original. Miles claimed Phelps to be a *quack, a charlatan* in the *New York Journal of Commerce*. Phelps countered with a published letter—*about as much claim to the title of doctor as my horse*. Miles pointing at the low price of Phelps' pill as evidence that no tomatoes were used to make them. Phelps calling Miles *unjust and unmanly*. For two years, the press happy to publish incredulous letters on tomato's healing power in exchange for tomato pill advertisement revenue. The public relished in the reading. The placebo effect? Americans chowing down on everything from tomato pies to soups to jams and jellies to ketchup. Changing my mind about simplicity, I'm at the kitchen window, dreaming of a grilled cheese, tomato, and basil sandwich, when the dog comes bounding through the backyard toward me, a dripping red ball in his mouth.

LABOR DAY

(with a line from Su Tung-P'o)

Men in yellow hardhats shouting. John Deere bulldozers and cranes and dump trucks. Steel striking steel—labor's bell. Giant root balls unearthed. Trees fall. Seagulls circle the earth's dark wound eager for the bodies of mice and moles. President Cleveland signed the law creating a national labor day: fair wages and hours, weekends, child labor laws, unions. My own father rising at dawn, putting on a blue collar to work on the freight trains he loved. Brotherhood of Railroad Trainmen. Strikes and family holdback at meals. My mother standing in line for a block of yellow government cheese, the powdered milk she used to stretch the gallon, an industrial can of peanut butter. When he died, the train stopped at the town's east-end depot. The crew walked the three miles to the funeral home and back to work. Engines roar; seagulls shriek. Shout answers shout.

men mimicking machines/engines purr, sputter, and stop/ pallbearers in blue

ECLIPSE

The sun has retreated behind the cloudbank,
crows from the shoulder.

Sky imitates the steel gray lake
and the horizon is lost in their mimicry.

Clouds of black nondescript birds swarm like locusts
moving from one abandoned cornfield to another.

Silhouettes of geese and ducks move across the slate sky,
black ghosts echoing the southern migration.

Tree skeletons hold forgotten nests up to them,
offerings they ignore.

I stand with my shadow
watching as the Earth swallows the full moon.

I walk back to the house alone.

common prayer

Shadows grow long at this hour.
Their language cool and dark.

Cows lie beneath the pasture tree —
a rest stop for the dead and the living.

NORTHERN LIGHTS

I step out the door
into the night,
into a world I no longer know,

or one stripped of the mind's veil.
A colossal snake,
green, iridescent,

its single eye a street lamp.
One-muscle being
moving in wavelike contractions

as it swallows the heavens.
Why are we so frightened of our own beauty?
Chameleons—ads in magazines,

on billboards—eat us alive,
spit a myth of mediocrity at us.
But I'm walking toward, and into

the serpent all at once,
my shadow hiding behind me.
If there is a God, please,

let just one man or woman wake
at this reptilian hour
to witness—

a lone woman
standing in the road,
the sky trembling before her.

RHODODENDRON, WINTER

after a photo by Emily Cross

A troupe of ghosts stand in abeyance—
radiant energy
we feel but cannot see.
A naive bud, abiding spring.
Gilded, like the age we live in—
a thin gold leaf of wealth for a few.
Greed, and fear of losing.
Leaves curl backwards into themselves,
exposing veins.
Darkness furthers isolation,
beast of winter.
This world has passed through
five mass extinctions
each one a distinct specter.
This world has returned from
five mass extinctions
each one a new blossoming.
Enter Homo sapiens—
roaming, foraging,
farming, manufacturing, digitizing.
Swift as gazelles,
overwhelming the waters,
plants, sentient beings.
Winter, the sixth,
lumbers toward us.
Who will witness the bloom?

DAILY BREAD

Outside my window
a barren field of snow blushes with the sunrise.

The shadow from the box elder slices
across the lean crust

and your dead body, decapitated
your nervous eyes and hopping and nibbling nature

devoured. Blood is barely spilled at 15 below,
just a fine dusting and the gorge, gaping and sanguine.

The tracks are quick and final
as a calligrapher's brushwork.

Yours like the face of a ghost
ambushed by the weasel's teeth and claws,

its belly and tail slipping silently out
from under the hemlock.

We all race
just one leap ahead of the darkness.

I get a shovel,
cover you with a sheet of snow,

cache the bounty for later.

LAID LOW WITH COVID, I PONDER THE LIGHTNING WHELK SHELL ON THE BOOKCASE

A carnivore adorned with lightning
stripes zigzagging from
each whorl of its shell.
The shell found in 6,000-year-old burial sites—
ceremonial drinking cup, beads,
tool for hammering.
Its whorl runs clockwise,
a staircase for the birth to death journey.
I am gripped by a red-crowned virus—
lungs filled with slime,
a wracking cough tears at my throat.
I am the clam
grabbed by the black beast,
shell strong as iron.
Pointed end jabbed between mine—
pushing,
patiently pushing.

MY MOTHER'S COAT

She fears her gray wool coat of 15 years won't survive
another winter. The top button went missing
who knows when. She thought about fixing
it, but one of her eight children lost
her button box in the woods, so she wears
a scarf. One hand beneath it for warmth, and worrying
the nub of threads. The bottom button fell off
last winter so she wears pants instead of skirts.
Snips the frayed hem and sleeves clean. When the lining
tears and falls apart, she gives up and decides
to cut the whole thing out, buttons the coat closed.
Checks it over daily for new signs of wear.
No one can see the inside—her heart,
racing like a rabbit startled by first snow.

RUE THIS DAY

Dead squirrel in the road.
Crows, crowding the corpse,
then rising, yakking it up—
winter's white noise.
Cars pass—
Ka thunk. Ka thunk. Ka thunk.
Two homeless guys at the hot bar
fill up on soup in one ounce tasting cups.
Ruta graveolons, common rue.
Not native here,
a shrubby plant, aromatic.
*Leaves taken with figs and walnuts
a counter-poison against the plague
and causes all venomous things to become harmless.*
What about this plague of hatred?
Possums are ugly and have scary teeth.
The guys at the hot bar—
can't they get a job?
First snow dusts the limbs of pine, hemlock,
freezes on the ferns in the understory.
But the great blue heron
down by the La Platte River marsh
lingers. Sandhill cranes too.
Like us, no urgency to migrate
yet. Four million years ago, tiny microbes
invisible to the naked eye
exhaled the oxygen that eight billion
of us inhale today.
How many of those lives do I see? See me?
Love me. Hate me. Either way.
My hands, the way I salt everything
on my plate, how I sing out of tune loudly
to the car radio, argue
with the crows at the feeder.
Love how I say *uman*, not *human*.
Save some part of this day
I have rued.

AT THE APPROACH OF THE WINTER SOLSTICE

It's possible the Pagans were right,
that the sun has stood still for 12 days,
and might not rise again.

It's 25 degrees below zero
and the world is curling into a fetal position.

Democracy, like the rest of us,
has been dying since the day of its birth,
and the snow blows sideways
through our dark days.

An ancient cause brought two strangers together.
Sitting knee to knee in the village square,
throughout the night,
they lit a log, and another,
and another.

Neither of them uttered a word
about the disagreement between heart and mind.
Through the eons it echoes.

MOURNING

Just before dawn
mourning doves under the feeders,
gleaning the snow for seed—
bodies like primitive gravestones.
I want to pick one up and
worry it in my hands—
feel the idea of cold granite
melt to warm silk of feathers.

So slow to startle.
My neighbor says
fat, stupid birds.
I think, too trusting,
no—lost,
lost in the desire for—
aware of the hawk's shadow
too late.
The bare grave.
The stone's imprint
filling with snow.

GOOD JOURNALISM TELLS US WHO, WHAT, WHEN, WHERE, AND WHY

Fool's spring. Sugar snow melts as it hits the ground. Flood watch. The river below the house swells, breaches. Wipes out the beaver dam. I stand on the bank waiting. For what? To see how they rebuild. Their inner life so simple—the dam. The lodge. Is this what makes courage possible? Out west biologists copy them, creating dams of mud and leaves and branches. To restore the floodplains. To hold back the wildfires. Quiet ways to save the burning world. But our orders were to *make some noise...some good trouble*. A student speaks to hold back the missiles firing. Who was detained? The hallowed halls recede into the shadows. Radio Static. Voice of America furloughed. Chilled speech. Guts of social security spill onto the rose garden lawn. Reading only the headlines, I cut the news accounts short like a guillotine. When Dorothy threw a bucket of water to save the scarecrow from the fire, the sodden witch cried, *I'm melting! Melting!* Dorothy claimed it was an accident. Down by the river, felled sumac and dogwood and birch. Beaver totems with pointed heads. A rusted sign post no longer a sign post. A red mitten hangs on it.

A PLEA

Driving down the hill this morning,
in the distance a cloudbank hangs
over Lake Champlain,
shoving the body of water against the small city.
Could be some beast's exhale.
Gray winter day—
pedestrians cross the street at the crosswalk,
crossing guards blow hot breath into their hands,
traffic lights change from yellow to red to green,
backpacks are shifted, slung, dragged.
Parents park their cars and hustle their children
towards the school's double doors.
No one's yelling, looks angry.
No one's looking up the weather on their phone.
Just shoulders hunched against the cold wind,
staring at the sidewalk.
I roll the window down and sigh,
and my breath floats into the frigid air
as a cumulus cloud.
Turning the news off,
I hear myself say:
O, America,
there is no beast.
It's just us—
trying not to fall through the cracks.

common prayer

At the horizon a gate opens
& the day slips through.

Not a moment between the dark and the light.

IN THE BEGINNING

there was the filament, a string
a double helix turning in on itself
reaching out of itself—
the universe
stitched together by a four-letter alphabet:
A, C, G, T.
Seeking an interpreter.

Is the world already made
or do we create it?
Here a tree.
There an apple.
My brother's fall from that building.

A is for asylum—Italians lift
Eritreans, Sudanese, Afghans
from the Mediterranean.
A woman grips a broken bowl
she's carried across the sea.

C is for children—52,000 breaching the border.

G is for genes—thousands each
carried by two billion people,
fleeing across continents.
They scuff a serpent's trail
through the shifting desert sands.

T is for turning against your own.

We are one part tree, one part apple,
one part serpent.
Turn us inside out
and the filament
threads itself with light,
mending the fractured vessel.

WE'VE LOST TRACK OF OUR MOTHER

Footprints, but no sign of her kerchief
knotted under her chin, her gray coat—
the one for best and worst, every day.
Where is she, if not just ahead of us,
clearing the snow from the path.

Who will toss the winds,
pull the tides from their slumber?

Black grackles light on the path,
pick at the crumbs—
their wings smeared with rainbows
occluded by our shadows.

Our weeping mother, full of grief—
we can't drink her waters.

Sand shifts at the bottom of the river,
carving a new channel—
an oxbow of separation.
Roots dangle from our tongues.

Who will lie with the beast,
calm our night terrors?

DIRGE

A flock of black back gulls on the pond.
Each one facing into the south wind—
dipping & preening,
rising to shudder themselves free.
They moan with pleasure in their morning bath.

I want to swallow one whole—
to know the moan
that begins at my navel
& fills my solar plexus.
To know the shudder,
beginning at the top of the head,
running like rapids through my body,
exiting at the tips of fingers & toes.
To cleanse myself of worry's dirge.

OUT OF SIGHT, OUT OF MIND

Straddling the wrack line—
the serpentine mass of kelp
at the high tide mark—
I pull a gull's primary feather
from a menagerie of plastic bottles,
cigarette butts, tampon tubes, a doll's head.

The feather needed for lift
and drag, forward thrust.

Above me a jet roars
and a stream of ice crystals
bloom and vanish.

Like this debris
carried out by the next tide.

BOOKMARK

I collect Tillandsia—air plants
thriving on the rain forest's dirty water
and filled with invisible creatures. Not distilled.
Like the truth I'm seeking.

I'm journeying the landscape
of family lore, filtered by shame,
embarrassment. Embellished
with hubris. Slogging through centuries,
bushwacking my way through war torn
countryside, the Jewish diaspora,
cobblestone and carriage.
All the while summoning the truth
within which lies myriad murmurs—
beguiling words devoured like
fairy tales over the millennia.

Tillandsia—belonging to the
pineapple family—600 plus members.
Unrooted, each one depends on
its curved leaves, like two hands
cupped to hold water.

My truth in family history
a bookmark.
Placing it between the pages,
10,000 stories shatter.
The wreckage quiet as the Green Mountains
left by a melting glacier.

TINY APOCALYPSE

It was the birdsong in the far away,
the snow-covered path shimmering
in the sunlight that eluded
what we came upon.
Our boots squeaking and crunching
along the frigid trail. Shadows
of bare trees crossing our path.
A closed gate we hiked our bodies over.
The rumble of railcars on the move somewhere
beyond the pine woods to the south.
Along the northern side, spiny buckthorn
where bluebirds, chickadees,
pine siskins, take cover.
The invasive buckthorn I loathe.
Suddenly a dribble of wood chips,
soon becoming shrapnel. Tree limbs
twisted and splintered, raw flesh exposed.
The brush hog, a ravaging ogre, having
wheeled its way through
tearing and ripping the invader
limb from limb.
Insatiable hunger. We wondered who
decides. The biologist says it depends
on habitat destruction. The utility arborist
notifies us of crews *performing vegetation management
next to the railroad tracks.*
And the birds?
I'm reminded of prehistoric
illustrations of a world without us.
Habitats shifting, plants and animals too.
Evolution's cleaver.
Time ticks. The sun goes down.
The tiny apocalypse shrouded in darkness.
We head back to the car, a fire in the woodstove,
food in the fridge, our made beds.

MEMORY'S MUSCLE

> *When man is gone and only gods remain*
> *To stride the world...*
> —Edna St. Vincent Millay, from
> *Epitaph for the Race of Man*

Just when I thought nothing of your world remained,
your last story a palimpsest on a shroud hung
out to dry, your sister Evelyn's screen door flung
wide and out stepped an elderly man talking plain—
he, one of those dozens of depression kids caught in the rain,
who found a home in your mother's barn among
the cows and chickens, learning to watch their tongue,
to do their chores, to go to school, to use their brain,
learning too that this world is not an empty shell
but a blue jewel floating among the stars,
and here in the fields and alleys and halls
memory's muscle never fails to foretell
that the gods who stride this earth no war
will ever make. Living is all.

PLOUGHSHARE TORTOISE

> *If you look closely enough, a tortoise is as magnificent as a tiger.*
> —Joel Sartore, author of *Photo Ark*

Knoxville Zoo a long way from Madagascar where the *golden tortoise* lives safely in captivity. No wildfires. No poachers. No high-end pet trade. Its gold carapace covered with a matrix of pentagons. A plough-shaped appendage under its neck. In Isaiah 2:4, the prophet urges people to *beat their swords into ploughshares and learn war no more.* More than 60 years ago the Soviet Union gifted the United Nations with the sculpture standing on the grounds today, depicting a man doing just that. Critically endangered. Functionally extinct in the wild. Prefers bamboo-scrub habitat. Endangered too. World's rarest tortoise. Rare as peace.

ADVOCATING FOR THE INCONCEIVEABLE

My everyday fears paralyzed me. Directions said to follow the trail along the La Platte River towards the lake. At the suspension bridge you will come upon a troll. Don't be frightened as it isn't real. Then the path will take you to some cliffs. There you will see where the water has fallen over the summit, descending over cracks and crevices, and frozen all the way to the ground before you. How it has melted and frozen again and again. Be like a cat (and there are many bobcats here) patiently watching and waiting for its prey, and you will see the ice disappearing. It will be like the day the mountains began walking.

water's steely scent/the sound of heavy footfall/finding my way home

a commoner's prayer

Today the pond at Meach Cove Farm is home to the cumulus clouds. Yesterday the great pines along the shoreline filled its rooms. My own body, a vessel filled with me; a house full of yearning. Some days I rest my chin on my hand, elbow on the desk and worry. Other days, I marvel at my fingers grasping and pulling weeds in the garden. Sometimes the north wind blows right through my body like those old farmhouses in the Northeast Kingdom where some women have reached beyond 100 years. Their harvest in and next year's seeds stored in glass jars on a shelf in the barn, they sit on the sofa in wool hats and coats, poking at a small fire in the woodstove. Recalling a photograph of one sitting next to a sow stretched out the length of the couch, its head filling her lap, I pray that I survive the wildfires and floods, the fall of democracy, and the home invasions that beset us, if only to know the warmth of such a beast and call it home.

dark days, blue sky days/the pond is never empty/where to rest my head

GONE

before I sat at this table pondering

before memes and hashtags and codes and AI

before trains, planes, and automobiles made the planet smaller

before oil rigs on the ocean and refineries in Houston

before plastic

before counting and zero and $E=mc^2$

before the plants and animals were named, classified, and reclassified

before we plowed the earth, built shelters and fences

before words and stories and believing

before fire

before we left the Great Rift valley

before Homo Sapiens

before Pangea and dinosaurs

before trilobites and horseshoe crabs

before the galaxy and our sun

before the Planck Epoch—that first fraction of a second after the Big Bang

then I understand the spill of rose petals on the ground

NOTES

"The Flower Carrier"
In 1935, Diego Rivera masterfully created The Flower Carrier (Cargador de Flores, oil and tempera on Masonite, 48 × 47 3/4 in.). The painting displays a peasant man in white clothing with a yellow sombrero, struggling on all fours with a dramatically oversized basket of flowers that is strapped to his back with a yellow sling. A woman, most likely the peasant's wife, stands behind him trying to help with the support of the basket as he attempts to rise to his feet.

"Translation"
The Cheryl Betz painting in oil and cold wax on canvas depicts a pine tree and, looking closely, wheeling through its high branches is a sea urchin. The oil and wax landscape paintings from the series Echinoides have linear elements repeatedly drawn into and onto the surfaces throughout many layers of paint application. This intermingling alters the narrative, pointing to the interconnection of all phenomena and to the impermanent nature of form, perception, and memory. The series is based on northeastern-coastal areas of the US, now threatened by our changing climate, that have had an impact on the artist.

"Monument"
Lines in italics are taken from a poem, author unknown, often read at Buddhist memorial services.

ACKNOWLEDGMENTS

My thanks to the editors of the following publications where these poems, sometimes in different versions, originally appeared:

Abstract Magazine, "Rhododendron, Winter"
The American Journal of Poetry, "In The Beginning"
Burningword Literary Review, "Small Histories"
Cider Press Review, "Northern Lights"
The Nature of our Times Anthology, "A Tree Treeing," "Ploughshare Tortoise"
Poem City Anthology 2023, "Migration"
Bearing Witness Anthology, "Good Journalism Tells Us Who, What, When, Where, and Why"
Walking Mountains, "Letter to Basho," "Letter to Cold Mountain"

A deep bow of gratitude to Janet Paulus for her insights on this manuscript, Meredith Markow for her monthly poems of encouragement, and Emily Cross for her photographic genius. Thank you Pine Street Poets, Sue Burton and Alison Prine, and remembering our dear Marylen Grigas. Without your enduring passion for poetry, your wisdom, and loving support this would not have been possible. I am also filled with joy for the new poetry friends in my life: Aylie Baker, Tanya Cimonetti, Jaina Clough, Camilla Rockwell, and Candelin Wahl. May we continue to grow together. Another deep bow to Hope Johnson, the Story family, and my Dharma brothers and sisters for their generosity. Not to forget! Samantha Kolber, publisher of Rootstock Publishing for choosing this manuscript. It has been great working with you!

ABOUT THE AUTHOR

Joan M. White's poems have been published in *Cider Press Review*, NPR's *On Being blog*, *Abstract Magazine*, and *Burningword Literary Journal*, among others. A practicing Zen Buddhist for more than thirty years, she is a student at the Vermont Zen Center where she edits the publication Walking Mountains, and offers seasonal workshops in haiku. She draws inspiration from her passion for and knowledge of plant life, wandering in the woods and wetlands, and reading about space/time. She lives in Shelburne, Vermont.

We Grow Our Books in Montpelier, Vermont

Learn more about our titles in Fiction, Nonfiction, Poetry and Children's Literature at the QR code below or visit www.rootstockpublishing.com.

www.ingramcontent.com/pod-product-compliance
Lightning Source LLC
LaVergne TN
LVHW091603060526
838200LV00036B/973